The Essential
FRENCH
COOKBOOK

The Essential
FRENCH
COOKBOOK

50 Classic Recipes, with Step-by-Step Photographs

Edited by Heather Thomas

COURAGE BOOKS

AN IMPRINT OF RUNNING PRESS
PHILADELPHIA • LONDON

Printed in Hong Kong

*This book may not be reproduced in whole or in part in any form or by
any means, electronic or mechanical, including photocopying, recording,
or by any information storage and retrieval system now known or here-
after invented, without written permission from the publisher.*

9 8 7 6 5 4 3 2 1

Digit on the right indicates the number of this printing

Library of Congress Cataloging-in-Publication Number
97-77960

ISBN 0-7624-0379-9

Designed and produced by SP Creative Design
Editor: Heather Thomas
Art Director: Al Rockall
Designer: Rolando Ugolini

Acknowledgements

Special photography: Laurie Evans
Step-by-step photography: GGS Photographics
Food preparation: Janice Murfitt and Dawn Stock

This book may be ordered by mail from the publisher.
But try your bookstore first!

Published by Courage Books, an imprint of
Running Press Book Publishers
125 South Twenty-second Street
Philadelphia, Pennsylvania 19103-4399

Notes

1. Standard spoon measurements are used in all recipes.

2. Eggs should be large unless otherwise stated.

3. Whole milk should be used unless otherwise stated.

4. Fresh herbs should be used unless otherwise stated.
If unavailable, use dried herbs as an alternative, but halve the
quantities stated.

5. Ovens should be preheated to the specified temperature.
If using a convection oven, follow the manufacturer's
instructions for adjusting the time and the temperature.

CONTENTS

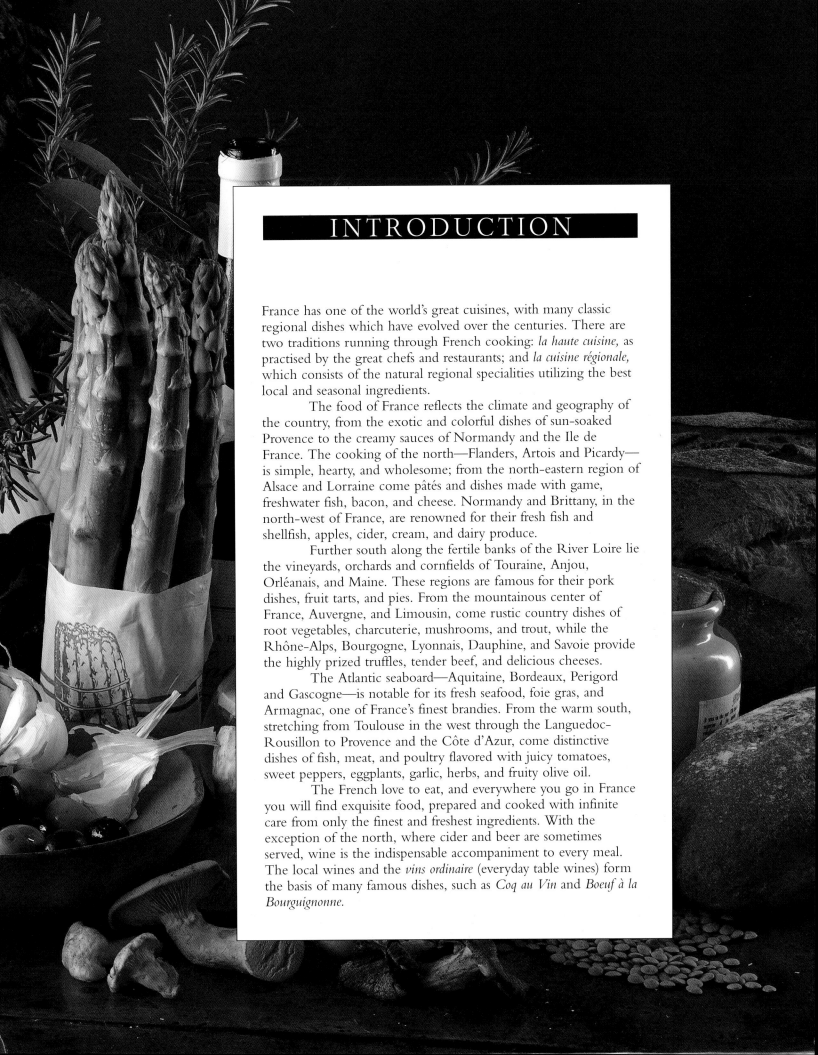

INTRODUCTION

France has one of the world's great cuisines, with many classic regional dishes which have evolved over the centuries. There are two traditions running through French cooking: *la haute cuisine,* as practised by the great chefs and restaurants; and *la cuisine régionale,* which consists of the natural regional specialities utilizing the best local and seasonal ingredients.

The food of France reflects the climate and geography of the country, from the exotic and colorful dishes of sun-soaked Provence to the creamy sauces of Normandy and the Ile de France. The cooking of the north—Flanders, Artois and Picardy— is simple, hearty, and wholesome; from the north-eastern region of Alsace and Lorraine come pâtés and dishes made with game, freshwater fish, bacon, and cheese. Normandy and Brittany, in the north-west of France, are renowned for their fresh fish and shellfish, apples, cider, cream, and dairy produce.

Further south along the fertile banks of the River Loire lie the vineyards, orchards and cornfields of Touraine, Anjou, Orléanais, and Maine. These regions are famous for their pork dishes, fruit tarts, and pies. From the mountainous center of France, Auvergne, and Limousin, come rustic country dishes of root vegetables, charcuterie, mushrooms, and trout, while the Rhône-Alps, Bourgogne, Lyonnais, Dauphine, and Savoie provide the highly prized truffles, tender beef, and delicious cheeses.

The Atlantic seaboard—Aquitaine, Bordeaux, Perigord and Gascogne—is notable for its fresh seafood, foie gras, and Armagnac, one of France's finest brandies. From the warm south, stretching from Toulouse in the west through the Languedoc-Rousillon to Provence and the Côte d'Azur, come distinctive dishes of fish, meat, and poultry flavored with juicy tomatoes, sweet peppers, eggplants, garlic, herbs, and fruity olive oil.

The French love to eat, and everywhere you go in France you will find exquisite food, prepared and cooked with infinite care from only the finest and freshest ingredients. With the exception of the north, where cider and beer are sometimes served, wine is the indispensable accompaniment to every meal. The local wines and the *vins ordinaire* (everyday table wines) form the basis of many famous dishes, such as *Coq au Vin* and *Boeuf à la Bourguignonne.*

Bouquet garni

This is a small bundle of herbs, usually sprigs of fresh parsley and thyme and a bay leaf, which are tied together with string or thread. It is used to flavor stocks, soups, stews, and casseroles and is immersed in the cooking liquid, and removed later before serving.

Cheeses

France is justly famous for its huge array of regional and locally produced cheeses of which there are literally hundreds. Each individual cheese has its own special texture, flavor, and character, which makes it unique. Cheeses are used in cooking, and the cheeseboard is an important ritual in most meals. It is

served before the dessert and a wide range of cheeses is offered. Some of the best-known French cheeses are as follows:

Brie: this is a creamy soft cheese from the Ile de France, which is best eaten when really ripe and runny.

Camembert: this soft cheese hails from Normandy and has a stronger flavor and aroma than Brie. It should also be served when it is ripe and is best consumed at room temperature, never straight out of the refrigerator.

Chèvre: most regions have their own local goat's milk cheeses, which are usually soft in texture with a strong distinctive flavor.

Gruyère: widely used in cooking, this cheese has a firm texture and a nutty, slightly salty flavor. It is made in the mountainous region of Savoie and is excellent for grating.

Roquefort: this is regarded by cheese afficionados as the king of cheeses. Blue-veined, semi-hard, with a creamy, crumbly texture, Roquefort is made from ewe's milk and is aged in the underground caves of the Saint-Affrique district in central France.

Confit d'oie

Traditionally used in cassoulet, this speciality of preserved goose, which has been cooked in goose fat, comes from south-western France. It can be purchased at most good delicatessens and specialist food stores.

Foie gras

This is held in high esteem by the French who regard it as the greatest of all culinary delicacies. *Foie gras* is the liver of specially fattened geese, and the finest ones come from Alsace and south-western France. The geese are fattened up in such a way that their livers grow to a considerable size. *Foie gras* is traditionally used in making pâté but it is also sometimes baked in brioche dough or used as a filling for crêpes and croquettes, or sliced and sautéed in butter.

Garlic

This is an essential ingredient in many French dishes, especially those of Provence and the south of the country. It is used as a flavoring in many soups, stews and casseroles, and is the essential ingredient in the great Provençal pistou sauce, which is stirred into a soup of beans and vegetables just before serving. Cut cloves of garlic are often rubbed around the inside of a salad bowl before adding the salad leaves to impart a subtle flavor and aroma to the salad. Likewise, they can be rubbed around an earthenware gratin dish before making a gratin of potatoes or other vegetables.

Herbs

Most savory dishes are flavored and scented with the aromatic leaves of at least one herb. Chervil, tarragon, parsley, and chives are the most frequently used ones, but rosemary, basil, and fennel are popular and, indeed, essential in many southern dishes. They may be tied together in a small bundle (*bouquet garni*) or chopped. They are added to omelets, sauces, soups, stews, casseroles, broiled meat, poultry, and fish. Fresh herbs are preferable to dried ones. You can buy them in most supermarkets or grow them yourself in your backyard or in pots on your kitchen windowsill.

Chives: the long onion-flavored leaves of chives are snipped with scissors and added to salads, omelets, soups, and sauces.

Parsley: sprigs may be used in a *bouquet garni*, or they can be chopped and used as a flavoring or as a garnish before serving.

Tarragon: this typically French herb is used to flavor many classic sauces, especially béarnaise sauce, omelets, and green salads. It can be steeped in wine vinegar to make *vinaigre à l'estragon*, which is used in sauces and salad dressings.

Thyme: the small leaves of this pungent herb are used for flavoring many soups, stews, and casseroles.

Mushrooms

In France, many varieties of mushrooms are used in cooking—not just the small cultivated button ones. Wild mushrooms are highly prized, especially *cèpes*, *chanterelles*, and *morilles* (morels). They are used in a wide range of dishes, and may be cooked in cream with herbs, or added to salads and sauces, or used as a filling for vol-au-vent cases and crêpes, or simply broiled or cooked *au gratin*.

Mustard

The most famous and widely used mustard is *moutarde de Dijon*, which is flavored with white wine and tarragon.

However, the mustards of Bordeaux and Meaux are also popular. Mustard is used as a flavoring in many sauces, and is mixed with olive oil and vinegar in salad dressings. All French mustards are sold ready mixed in bottles as a paste, not in powdered form.

Olive oil

This is made by pressing ripe olives and is essential for making authentic vinaigrette salad dressings, mayonnaise, *aioli*, and *rouille*. Olive oil is an essential ingredient in many dishes from Provence, unlike the cookery of the north where butter is widely used instead. The finest and purest oil is extracted cold from the best ripe olives and is green and fruity. However, it is expensive and you can buy cheaper alternatives, although they will not have the same flavor and aroma.

Olives

These are characteristic of southern French cookery, and are used in many ways: as a garnish, in stuffings and sauces, and most notably in *tapenade* and *daubes*, the distinctive stews of Provence.

Onions

These deserve a special mention because they are used so extensively in French cookery: in sauces, tarts, casseroles, stews, and classic dishes such as *soupe à l'oignon* and *pissaladière*. A variety of onions are used from the tiny pickling onions and shallots to large mild onions, red skinned ones, and the tender shoots of scallions.

Snails

Known in France as *escargots*, snails can be cooked fresh in wine or broth with various herbs, scallions, and vegetables for flavoring, but they are usually

purchased canned or frozen and are packed into shells with garlic or herb butter before heating and serving as an hors d'œuvre.

Wine

Wine is the natural partner of good food, and many of the world's finest wines come from France. It is an essential ingredient in many French regional dishes, but you need not use really expensive wine for cooking. A bottle of inexpensive *vin ordinaire* is usually suitable although some leftover good wine will elevate many dishes into new realms *par excellence!*

Equipment and utensils

There are a few basic items that are very useful when cooking French food. These include the following:

Bain-marie: this is a large shallow pan in which saucepans, bowls or dishes can be placed in a bath of water. The water should come halfway up the sides of the pan or dish. It is ideal for making sauces and egg custards and prevents them curdling.

Casserole: this may be earthenware (for using in the oven) or cast iron (for cooking on top of the stove). It is ideal for making stews and *daubes*. A flameproof casserole is excellent for frying vegetables and meat on top of the stove, before adding the cooking liquid and placing in the oven for long, slow cooking.

Omelet pan: a small pan with sloping sides for making crêpes and omelets. It may be made of copper, cast iron, steel, or aluminum.

Soufflé dish: this high-sided fluted dish is usually made of white porcelain and can be used for making hot or cold soufflés.

ESCARGOTS A L'ALSACIENNE

Snails Alsace-style

1 Remove the snails from the can. Heat 2 tablespoons of the butter in a skillet and quickly fry the snails. Add the wine and cook over high heat for 2–3 minutes until it evaporates. Add the stock and boil for 2 minutes. Leave to cool and then remove the snails. Discard the stock.

3 Carefully put a little of the garlic and herb flavored butter into each snail shell. Then put a snail inside each shell and cover with a little more of the garlic butter.

2 Cream the remaining butter in a small bowl. Mix in the garlic, chopped parsley and onion, and the hazelnuts. Season with salt and freshly ground black pepper.

PREPARATION: 20 MINUTES
COOKING: 10 MINUTES
SERVES: 6

36 canned snails and 36 shells
2/3 cup butter
3 tablespoons dry white wine
1/2 cup chicken stock
4 garlic cloves, minced
bunch of parsley, finely chopped
1/4 cup finely chopped onion
1/2 cup hazelnuts, crushed
salt and freshly ground black pepper

4 Arrange all the filled snail shells on special snail dishes or in an ovenproof dish, and bake in a preheated oven at 400° for 10 minutes. Serve immediately.

PISSALADIERE

Provençal onion and anchovy tart

1 Make the dough: dissolve the yeast in the water and set aside. Sift the flour and salt into a large mixing bowl, rub in the butter and make a well in the center. Mix in the eggs and yeast liquid, drawing in the flour from the sides of the bowl to make a soft dough.

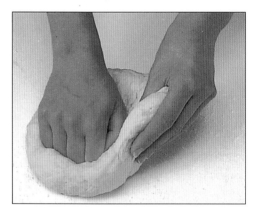

2 Turn onto a floured surface and knead until smooth and elastic. Form into a ball, cover with a damp cloth and leave to rise in a warm place for 30–45 minutes, until doubled in bulk. Meanwhile, heat 4 tablespoons of the oil and cook the onions gently for about 30 minutes until soft and golden.

PREPARATION: 30 MINUTES +
RESTING TIME
COOKING: 30 MINUTES
SERVES: 6–8

3 Knock down the risen dough and knead again for a few minutes. Roll out to a circle to fit an oiled 10-inch round ovenproof plate, baking pan or mold and use to line the base. Spread the onions over the top.

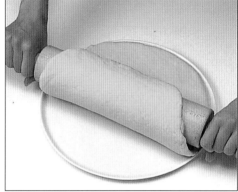

| 6 tablespoons olive oil |
| 2 pounds onions, thinly sliced |
| 12 canned anchovies, drained |
| 1/2 cup ripe olives, halved and pitted |
| freshly ground black pepper |
| **For the dough:** |
| 1 cake compressed yeast |
| 4 tablespoons lukewarm water |
| 3 cups all-purpose flour |
| pinch of salt |
| 1/4 cup butter, diced |
| 2 eggs, beaten |

4 Make a lattice pattern with the anchovies over the onions and decorate with the olives. Sprinkle with pepper and the remaining oil. Leave to rise in a warm place for 15 minutes. Bake in a preheated oven at 450° for 30 minutes.

PATE DE CAMPAGNE

French country pâté

1 Melt the butter in a skillet and sauté the onions and garlic gently for a few minutes, until tender and golden. Transfer to a large bowl. Add the liver to the skillet and fry until lightly browned. Remove and grind or chop.

2 Chop 7 ounces of the bacon and add to the bowl with the liver, pork, parsley, sage, mace, nutmeg, salt, pepper, egg whites, and brandy. Mix well until thoroughly combined.

¼ cup butter, plus extra for greasing
2 onions, finely chopped
4 garlic cloves, minced
1 pound pig's liver, diced
9 ounces bacon slices, rind removed
1 pound lean pork, ground or chopped
2 tablespoons chopped fresh parsley
½ teaspoon dried sage
¼ teaspoon ground mace
¼ teaspoon ground nutmeg
salt and freshly ground black pepper
2 egg whites
2 tablespoons brandy
2 bay leaves

4 Leave the pâté to cool for 30 minutes, then cover with a piece of waxed paper or foil and weight lightly. Leave until completely cold and set. If wished, replace the bay leaves with fresh ones. Cover and refrigerate for about 36 hours. Serve sliced with toast or crusty bread.

3 Line a lightly greased 1-pound terrine or loaf pan with the remaining bacon slices so that they hang over the sides. Fill with the pâté mixture and fold the bacon over the top. Put the 2 bay leaves on top and place in a roasting pan of hot water. Cook in a preheated oven at 375° for 1½ hours, or until the juices run clear and the pâté has shrunk slightly from the sides of the pan.

PREPARATION: 30 MINUTES
COOKING: 1½ HOURS
SERVES: 8

FLAMICHE AUX POIREAUX

Leek pie

1 Make the *pâte brisée*: sift the flour and salt into a large mixing bowl. Cut the butter into small dice and rub into the flour until the mixture resembles bread crumbs. Stir in the egg yolk and sufficient iced water to bind the ingredients together.

3 Melt the butter in a heavy pan and cook the leeks very gently until soft and melting; this takes about 30 minutes. Stir occasionally. Add the nutmeg and seasoning and leave to cool. Whisk together the egg yolks and cream and stir into the cooled leeks.

¹/₄ cup butter
2 pounds leeks, thinly sliced
pinch of ground nutmeg
salt and pepper
3 egg yolks
¹/₂ cup heavy cream
For the *pâte brisée*:
3 cups all-purpose flour
pinch of salt
³/₄ cup butter
1 egg yolk
4–6 tablespoons iced water
For the glaze:
1 egg yolk
1 tablespoon water

4 Pour the leek filling into the pastry shell. Roll out the remaining pastry to make a lid. Moisten the edges and cover the flan. Pinch the edges together to seal, and crimp with a fork. Decorate with leaves made from the pastry trimmings. Beat the egg yolk and water together and brush over the pastry. Bake in a preheated oven at 400° for 35–40 minutes.

2 Knead lightly on a floured surface until smooth and elastic. Cover and leave in a cool place to rest for 1 hour. Roll out two-thirds of the pastry on a floured surface and use to line a buttered 9-inch quiche pan placed on a greased baking sheet.

PREPARATION: 50 MINUTES + RESTING TIME
COOKING: 35–40 MINUTES
SERVES: 6

CROQUETTES DE CAMEMBERT
Camembert fritters

1 Remove the rind from the Camembert cheese. Mash the cheese with a fork in a small bowl and beat well until it is really smooth.

2 Make a *roux*: melt the butter in a saucepan and stir in the flour. Cook for 1–2 minutes without browning and then stir in the milk and brandy or Calvados, beating vigorously to make a smooth, thick sauce. Season with pepper and cool. Mix in the Camembert to make a firm croquette mixture.

3 Take small amounts of the cheese mixture and roll between floured hands to make cork-shaped croquettes. Beat the egg with 2 tablespoons of cold water and use to coat the croquettes.

4 Roll the croquettes at once in a mixture of flour and bread crumbs and then deep-fry them quickly in hot oil until golden brown. Drain on absorbent paper towels and serve garnished with sprigs of parsley.

PREPARATION: 12–15 MINUTES
COOKING: 15–20 MINUTES
SERVES: 4

1 Camembert cheese, just ripe
1 tablespoon butter
1/4 cup flour
5 tablespoons warm milk
1 tablespoon brandy or Calvados
1/4 teaspoon freshly ground white pepper
1 egg
1 tablespoon flour and 3 tablespoons dry bread crumbs for coating
oil for deep-frying
To garnish:
sprigs of parsley

SOUPE A L'OIGNON

French onion soup

1 Melt the butter in a large saucepan and add the onions and sugar. Lower the heat to a bare simmer and cook the onions very slowly for 20–30 minutes until they are soft and a really deep golden brown. Stir occasionally and take care that they cook to a good color without burning.

2 Stir the flour into the onion mixture and cook over a very low heat for about 5 minutes, stirring well to prevent it burning or sticking to the bottom of the pan.

3 Add the beef stock and the salt and freshly ground black pepper. Turn up the heat and bring to a boil, stirring. Reduce the heat and simmer for 15–20 minutes. Taste the soup and add more salt and freshly ground black pepper if necessary.

4 Meanwhile, toast the slices of French bread lightly on both sides. Sprinkle with the grated Swiss cheese. Pour the soup into a hot tureen. Place a piece of toast in each serving bowl and ladle the hot soup over the top.

¹/₄ cup butter
1¹/₂ pounds onions, thinly sliced
2 teaspoons sugar
2 teaspoons all-purpose flour
4¹/₂ cups beef stock
salt and freshly ground black pepper
¹/₂ French bread stick, sliced
¹/₄ cup grated Swiss cheese

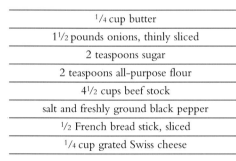

PREPARATION: 15 MINUTES
COOKING: 1 HOUR
SERVES: 4–5

POTAGE SAINT-GERMAIN
Split pea soup

1 Place the split peas in a sieve or a colander and rinse them thoroughly under running cold water. Soak them in cold water overnight, then rinse and drain.

2 Fry the strips of pork in the butter in a large heavy saucepan. Cook over a brisk heat for 5 minutes, stirring frequently. Add the carrot and onion and fry for a further 2 minutes, stirring constantly. Add the water and split peas and bring to the boil. Tie the bay leaves and celery together and lower into the pan with the garlic. Season and simmer very gently for 2 hours.

PREPARATION: 10–15 MINUTES +
SOAKING OVERNIGHT
COOKING: 2¼ HOURS
SERVES: 6

3 Discard the bay leaves and garlic. Purée the soup in a food processor or blender until it is thick and smooth—you will have to do this in batches. Return the puréed soup to the saucepan.

4 Stir in the cream and cook very gently over a low heat for a few minutes to heat through. Stir constantly and take care that the soup does not boil. Taste and adjust the seasoning if necessary. Pour into a warm tureen or individual bowls and serve garnished with croûtons.

2 cups dried yellow split peas
¼ pound boneless salt pork, cut in strips
2 tablespoons butter
1 carrot, diced
1 onion, chopped
9 cups water
2 bay leaves
1 celery stick
1 garlic clove, peeled and bruised
salt and freshly ground black pepper
½ cup heavy cream
To garnish:
bread croûtons

SOUPE AU PISTOU

Vegetable soup with basil sauce

1 Put the beans in a large bowl and cover with cold water. Leave overnight or for at least 5 hours to soak. Drain the beans and transfer to a saucepan. Cover with fresh water and bring to a boil. Skim off any scum on the surface and boil for 10 minutes. Reduce the heat and simmer for 1 hour, or until tender. Drain and set aside.

2 Prepare all the vegetables: dice the carrots, leeks, and celery. Skin and roughly chop the tomatoes. Peel and dice the potatoes. Top and tail the beans and cut them into 1/2-inch lengths. Trim and dice the zucchini.

3 Heat the olive oil in a large saucepan and add the carrots, leeks, celery, and tomatoes. Cook gently for 2 minutes, and then add the water. Bring to a boil, then reduce the heat immediately and simmer for 15 minutes. Add the potatoes, beans, zucchini, and vermicelli. Simmer for 15–20 minutes, until the pasta and all the vegetables are tender. Season with salt and pepper.

1 1/4 cups dried haricot beans
1/2 pound carrots
2 leeks
2 sticks celery
3/4 pound tomatoes
1/2 pound potatoes
1/2 pound thin green beans
3/4 pound zucchini
2 tablespoons olive oil
5 cups water
2 ounces vermicelli
salt and freshly ground black pepper

For the *pistou*:

3–4 garlic cloves, peeled
pinch of salt
20 large basil leaves
1 cup grated Parmesan cheese
1/2 cup olive oil

4 Make the *pistou*: pound the garlic cloves, salt, and basil in a blender or food processor. Add the Parmesan and then pour in the olive oil in a thin trickle through the feed tube until you have a thick green paste. Stir into the soup just before serving, or serve the *pistou* separately.

PREPARATION: 1 1/2 HOURS + SOAKING TIME
COOKING: 35–40 MINUTES
SERVES: 6

TARTE A L'OIGNON

Onion tart

1 Heat the butter in a large skillet. Add the bacon and onions and fry gently over a low heat until soft and golden. Add the flour and cook for 1 minute. Stir in the milk and cream and cook for 5 minutes, stirring occasionally.

2 Remove the skillet from the heat and add the egg yolks, salt, freshly ground black pepper, and some ground nutmeg. Stir well and then set aside to cool.

3 Roll out the *pâte brisée* (shortcrust pastry) on a lightly floured surface and use to line a buttered 10-inch loose-bottomed quiche pan. Prick the base of the pastry with a fork.

¼ cup butter
¾ cup diced bacon
1 pound onions, finely sliced
¼ cup all-purpose flour
¾ cup milk
6 tablespoons light cream
2 egg yolks
salt and freshly ground black pepper
pinch of ground nutmeg
½ pound *pâte brisée* (see page 110)

4 Pour the prepared onion mixture into the pastry shell. Slide on to a cookie sheet and cook in a preheated oven at 350° for 40 minutes, until set and golden. Serve hot.

PREPARATION: 30 MINUTES
COOKING: 40 MINUTES
SERVES: 6

SOUFFLE AU FROMAGE

Cheese soufflé

1 Make a white sauce: melt the butter in a saucepan and stir in the flour. Cook for 1–2 minutes over a low heat and then gradually add the milk, stirring well between each addition, until the sauce is thick and smooth. Cook very gently for 15 minutes, stirring constantly with a wooden spoon. Remove from the heat and stir in the cream.

3 Whisk the egg whites in a clean bowl until they are really stiff, but not dry. Fold them gently into the cheese sauce mixture with a metal spoon using a figure-eight motion.

¼ cup butter
½ cup all-purpose flour
1 cup milk
2 tablespoons cream
4 egg yolks, beaten
1½ cups grated Swiss cheese
salt and freshly ground white pepper
pinch of ground nutmeg
5 egg whites

2 Stir the egg yolks into the sauce, a little at a time. Add the Swiss cheese, salt, pepper, and nutmeg to taste. Beat well until the cheese melts and the mixture is really smooth.

PREPARATION: 20 MINUTES
COOKING: 30 MINUTES
SERVES: 4

4 Transfer the mixture to a well-buttered 2-pint soufflé dish or two 1-pint dishes. Bake in a preheated oven at 350° for 15 minutes. Increase the temperature to 400° and cook for a further 15 minutes until the soufflé is well-risen and golden. Serve immediately.

QUICHE LORRAINE
Savory bacon tart

2 cups all-purpose flour
pinch of salt
½ cup butter
1 egg yolk
2–3 tablespoons iced water
For the filling:
¼ cup butter
1 cup diced bacon
1½ cups heavy cream
3 eggs
¼ teaspoon ground nutmeg
salt and freshly ground black pepper

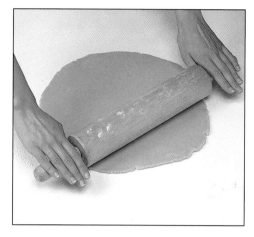

2 Roll out the pastry on a lightly floured surface and use to line a buttered 9-inch loose-bottomed quiche pan. Prick the base of the pastry shell with a fork.

3 Melt half of the butter in a skillet and cook the bacon gently until lightly colored. Put the cream and eggs in a bowl and whisk together. Add the nutmeg and seasoning.

1 Make the pastry: sift the flour and salt into a large mixing bowl and rub in the butter until the mixture resembles bread crumbs. Mix in the egg yolk and sufficient iced water to bind the ingredients. Knead the dough lightly and then chill in the refrigerator for 30 minutes.

4 Sprinkle the cooked bacon over the base of the pastry shell and dot with the remaining butter. Pour in the cream and egg mixture. Bake in a preheated oven at 400° for 30 minutes, or until set and golden brown. Serve warm.

PREPARATION: 20 MINUTES +
30 MINUTES CHILLING TIME
COOKING: 30 MINUTES
SERVES: 6

PIPERADE

Hot sweet pepper omelet

3 Beat the eggs together lightly in a bowl. Pour the beaten eggs into a lightly oiled or greased skillet and cook for 2–3 minutes over a very low heat without stirring.

1 Roast the sweet red peppers under a preheated hot broiler until the skins become charred, turning them frequently. Remove from the heat and place in a polythene bag for a few minutes (this makes it easier to remove the skins). Remove from the bag and skin the peppers. Cut in half and remove the ribs and seeds. Slice the flesh thinly.

4 large sweet red peppers
7 tablespoons olive oil
4 large onions, thinly sliced
1 hot pimiento, thinly sliced
2 garlic cloves, minced
pinch of sugar
2 pounds tomatoes, skinned, seeded and chopped
1 *bouquet garni*
salt and freshly ground black pepper
6 thick slices ham, preferably Bayonne
6 eggs

2 Heat 6 tablespoons of oil in a skillet, add the sweet pepper strips and sauté over medium heat until soft, stirring frequently. Add the onions, pimiento, and garlic and fry gently for 10 minutes, stirring. Add the sugar, tomatoes, *bouquet garni*, and seasoning. Cook gently for a further 10 minutes, stirring occasionally. Heat the ham gently in a separate skillet with the remaining oil.

4 Remove the *bouquet garni* from the vegetable mixture, and stir into the eggs. Keep stirring until the eggs start to scramble and cook through. Adjust the seasoning to taste. Serve the *pipérade* straight from the skillet accompanied by the slices of ham.

PREPARATION: 15–20 MINUTES
COOKING: 25–30 MINUTES
SERVES: 6

CREPES DE FRUITS DE MER
Seafood crêpes

1 Make the crêpes: sift the flour and salt into a mixing bowl and make a well in the center. Break in the eggs and add some of the milk. Beat in the flour from the sides of the bowl to make a thick batter. Gradually beat in the remaining milk until the batter is really smooth.

2 Heat a little butter in a small skillet and pour in sufficient batter to cover the base, tilting the skillet. Cook until the underside is golden brown and then flip the crêpe over and cook the other side. Slide out on to a warm plate and make the other crêpes in the same way. Keep warm.

PREPARATION: 20 MINUTES
COOKING: 45 MINUTES
SERVES: 4–6

3 Make the filling: put the fish in a saucepan with the wine and poach gently for 10 minutes. Add the scallops and cook for 2–3 minutes. Drain, reserving the liquor. Melt the butter in a small saucepan and fry the onion until golden. Add the mushrooms, fry for 2 minutes and stir in the flour. Cook for 1 minute and add the reserved fish liquor. Bring to the boil and cook for 2 minutes, stirring. Add the cream, fish, scallops, shrimp, the seasoning, and lemon juice.

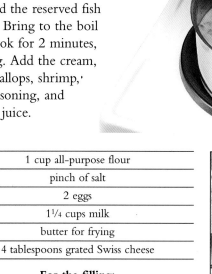

1 cup all-purpose flour
pinch of salt
2 eggs
1¼ cups milk
butter for frying
4 tablespoons grated Swiss cheese
For the filling:
½ pound angler fish, dog fish, or cod, skinned and boned
⅔ cup dry white wine
4 scallops, shucked
¼ cup butter
1 onion, finely chopped
1 cup chopped mushrooms
¼ cup all-purpose flour
⅔ cup crème fraîche or heavy cream
¼ pound peeled cooked shrimp
salt and freshly ground black pepper
1 teaspoon lemon juice

4 Place some of the seafood filling on each crêpe and roll up. Arrange the crêpes in a buttered ovenproof dish and sprinkle the grated cheese over the top. Bake in a preheated oven at 400° for 8–10 minutes until golden brown.

GOUGERE

Savory choux ring

1 cup all-purpose flour
3 medium eggs, beaten
⅓ cup butter
1 cup water
⅓ cup grated Swiss cheese
salt and pepper
pinch of cayenne pepper
2 ounces Swiss cheese, cut into small dice

2 Immediately tip the flour, all at once, into the pan. Remove from the heat and beat well with a wooden spoon until it forms a ball and leaves the sides of the pan clean. Allow to cool for a few minutes.

3 Gradually add the beaten eggs, a little at a time, beating well between each addition. Beat in ¼ cup of the grated Swiss cheese and then add the salt, pepper, and cayenne. Lastly, gently fold in the diced Swiss cheese.

1 Sieve the flour at least twice. This is very important if you are to be successful. If there is the slightest lump, you will not lose it in the choux pastry mixture. Put the butter and water in a medium-sized saucepan and bring to a full, rolling boil.

4 Drop tablespoonfuls of the mixture in a circle, but not quite touching, on a greased cookie sheet. Sprinkle with the remaining grated cheese and then bake in a preheated oven at 425° for 25–30 minutes, until well-risen, crisp and golden brown. Cool for a few minutes before serving.

PREPARATION: 15 MINUTES
COOKING: 25–30 MINUTES
SERVES: 4

BOURRIDE

Fish stew

1 Make the *court bouillon*: put the water, white wine, onion, leek, lemon, herbs, fish trimmings, salt, and peppercorns into a large saucepan. Bring to a boil and then simmer for 45 minutes. Strain the *court bouillon* into a clean saucepan.

2 Put the pieces of fish and the potatoes into the strained *court bouillon*. Cover the pan and bring to a boil. Reduce the heat and then simmer gently for 15 minutes, or until the fish and potatoes are cooked. Remove with a slotted spoon and transfer to a deep dish or tureen.

3 Measure the *court bouillon* and, if necessary, make it up to 2½ cups with water. Beat the egg yolks into ¾ cup of the *aioli*. Add a little of the *court bouillon* and blend well together.

2 pounds firm white fish, trimmed and cut into large pieces
1 pound firm potatoes, peeled and thickly sliced
2 egg yolks
1¼ cups *aioli* (see page 110)
6–8 slices French bread, toasted or fried
2 tablespoons chopped fresh parsley

For the *court bouillon*:

2½ cups water
⅔ cup dry white wine
1 onion, sliced
1 leek, trimmed and sliced
1 slice of lemon
1 sprig of parsley
1 sprig of thyme
1 sprig of fennel
¾ pound fish trimmings
1 teaspoon salt
6 black peppercorns

4 Return to the pan with the rest of the *court bouillon* and cook gently over a low heat, stirring all the time, until the sauce is thick enough to coat the back of a spoon. Pour the sauce over the fish and potatoes. To serve, place 1–2 slices of French bread in each hot soup plate. Arrange some fish and potatoes in their sauce on top. Sprinkle with chopped parsley and serve the remaining *aioli* separately.

PREPARATION: 30 MINUTES
COOKING: 1¼–1½ HOURS
SERVES: 4–6

QUENELLES AVEC CREVETTES
Quenelles in shrimp sauce

10 ounces white fish fillets, e.g. sole, flounder
salt and freshly ground black pepper
good pinch of ground nutmeg
½ cup heavy cream
1 egg, plus 1 egg white
For the sauce:
½ pound cooked shrimp in their shells
1²/₃ cups water
2 tablespoons butter
2 tablespoons flour
1 tablespoon tomato paste
½ teaspoon sugar
⅓ cup light cream
¼ cup Madeira
salt and pepper
To garnish:
sprigs of fresh dill weed

2 Meanwhile, make the sauce: peel the shrimp, cut into small pieces and set aside. Place the shells in a small saucepan with the water. Cover and simmer for 25–30 minutes. Liquidize the shells and liquid, and push them through a sieve.

1 Cut the fish fillets into pieces, discarding any skin and bones. Process to a smooth purée in a food processor or blender. Add the seasoning, nutmeg, cream, egg, and egg white, and process for about 30 seconds until thick and creamy. Chill in the refrigerator for at least 1 hour.

PREPARATION: 10 MINUTES +
1 HOUR CHILLING TIME
COOKING: 1 HOUR
SERVES: 4

3 Heat the butter in a clean small saucepan and stir in the flour. Cook gently for 2 minutes without browning. Add the sieved shell liquid and stir over a low heat until you have a smooth sauce. Simmer gently for 12–14 minutes and then add the tomato paste, sugar, and cream. Simmer gently for 5 minutes, add the Madeira and seasoning. Stir in the reserved shrimp.

4 Bring a large saucepan of salted water to a boil and then reduce the heat to a simmer. Slide tablespoons of the quenelle mixture into the simmering water. Cook gently for about 5 minutes, until set and cooked. Remove with a slotted spoon and keep warm while you cook the rest. Serve the quenelles in a pool of shrimp sauce garnished with sprigs of dill weed.

41

FILETS DE SOLE A LA NORMANDE
Normandy-style sole

4 soles, about 11 ounces each, filleted
1 onion, thinly sliced
2 carrots, thinly sliced
1 *bouquet garni*
1½ cups water
1¼ cups dry white wine
salt and freshly ground black pepper
⅔ cup butter
¼ pound button mushrooms
1 tablespoon lemon juice
4 cups fresh mussels in their shells
1 onion, finely chopped
2 egg yolks
¾ cup heavy cream
¼ cup shelled cooked shrimp

To garnish:

2 tablespoons chopped fresh parsley

2 Season the sole fillets with salt and pepper. Melt 2 tablespoons of the butter in a flameproof casserole, add the sole fillets and mushrooms, sprinkle with lemon juice, and strain the fish stock over the top. Cover and bake in a preheated oven at 350° for 12–15 minutes, until tender. Remove the sole and mushrooms and keep warm. Keep the stock.

1 Make the fish stock: put any skin and bones (and fish heads if available) from the sole in a large saucepan with the onion, carrots, *bouquet garni*, water, and ¾ cup of the white wine. Bring to a boil, then reduce the heat, cover the pan and simmer for 20 minutes.

PREPARATION: 15 MINUTES
COOKING: 1 HOUR
SERVES: 6

3 Wash and scrub the mussels and discard any that are open or cracked. Put them in a large saucepan with the onion and the remaining wine. Cook over a high heat until the shells open, shaking the pan. Discard any that do not open. Remove half of the mussels from their shells. Keep all the mussels warm.

4 Strain the cooking juices from the mussels and sole into a pan and boil steadily until reduced by three-quarters. Remove from the heat. Mix together the egg yolks and cream and stir into the cooking juices. Stir constantly over a low heat for 3–4 minutes, without boiling. Remove from the heat again, and whisk in the remaining butter, a little at a time. Pour the sauce over the sole, shelled mussels, and the shrimp. Garnish with the mussels in their shells and sprinkle with parsley.

LOUP EN FENOUIL

Charcoal-broiled sea bass with fennel

1 Sprinkle the sea bass with 3 tablespoons of the olive oil and season inside and out with salt and freshly ground black pepper. Stuff the dried fennel stalks inside the fish, and place on a grid over glowing hot charcoal or under a preheated moderate broiler. Cook the bass for 25–30 minutes, turning the fish over carefully halfway through cooking.

3 Meanwhile, make the sauce: put the egg yolks in a bowl with the prepared mustard and some salt and freshly ground black pepper. Mix well. Whisk in the oil, a few drops at a time initially and then in a thin steady stream when the sauce starts to emulsify. Whisk vigorously all the time until the sauce thickens.

1 x 2-pound sea bass, cleaned
6 tablespoons olive oil
salt and freshly ground black pepper
few dried fennel stalks
1 large fennel bulb, chopped
2 tablespoons crushed red peppercorns
For the sauce:
2 egg yolks
1 teaspoon prepared French mustard
1¼ cups olive oil
2 tablespoons vinegar
2 sweet dill pickles, drained and finely chopped
1 tablespoon drained capers, finely chopped
1 tablespoon chopped fresh parsley
1 tablespoon snipped chives

PREPARATION: 15 MINUTES
COOKING: 25–30 MINUTES
SERVES: 4

2 Heat the remaining olive oil in a small saucepan and add the chopped fennel. Sauté over gentle heat, stirring occasionally, until the fennel is really soft and golden. Season with salt and freshly ground black pepper and keep warm.

4 When the sauce is thick, whisk in the vinegar until thoroughly incorporated. Stir in the sweet dill pickles, capers, and herbs, and season to taste. Serve the fish, cut into 4 portions, with the sautéed fennel. Sprinkle with crushed red peppercorns and serve the sauce separately.

TRUITES AUX AMANDES

Trout with almonds

4 trout, about ¹/₂ pound each
³/₄ cup milk
1 tablespoon all-purpose flour
1 tablespoon oil
²/₃ cup butter
salt and freshly ground black pepper
1 cup slivered almonds
To garnish:
lemon quarters
2 tablespoons finely chopped parsley

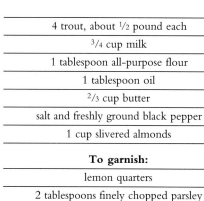

1 Clean and wash the trout under cold running water. Pat dry with absorbent paper towels. Put the milk in one dish and the flour in another. Dip each trout into the milk and then coat with flour. Shake gently to remove any excess flour.

2 Heat the oil and ¹/₂ cup of the butter in a large heavy skillet. Add the trout and cook gently for about 5 minutes on each side until cooked and golden brown. Take care that the butter does not burn. Remove and place on a warmed serving dish. Sprinkle with salt and pepper and keep the trout warm.

3 Wash out the skillet and dry thoroughly. Add the remaining butter and heat gently until the butter starts to foam.

4 Add the almonds and cook over a moderate heat for about 2 minutes, stirring constantly, until golden all over. Sprinkle the almonds and the butter over the trout, and serve immediately, garnished with lemon quarters and sprinkled with parsley.

PREPARATION: 10 MINUTES
COOKING: 12 MINUTES
SERVES: 4

BOUILLABAISSE

Fish stew from Marseilles

¾ cup olive oil
2 onions, thinly sliced
2 leeks, trimmed and thinly sliced
3 tomatoes, skinned, seeded and chopped
4 garlic cloves, minced
1 sprig of fennel
1 sprig of thyme
1 bay leaf
1 strip orange peel, without pith
1½ pounds shellfish, e.g. crab, mussels, jumbo shrimp
9 cups boiling water
salt and freshly ground black pepper
5 pounds fish, e.g. angler fish, bass, dog fish
4 pinches of saffron powder
To serve:
slices of hot toast
1¼ cups *rouille* (see page 110)

2 Add the shellfish, boiling water, and some salt and freshly ground black pepper to the pan. Turn up the heat and boil for about 3 minutes to allow the oil and water to combine.

4 When the fish is cooked, taste the *bouillabaisse* and adjust the seasoning. Stir in the powdered saffron and then pour into a warmed tureen or soup dishes. Serve immediately with slices of hot toast topped with a spoonful of rouille.

3 Add your chosen fish to the saucepan and reduce the heat. Continue cooking over a medium heat for 12–15 minutes, until cooked. The fish should be opaque and tender but still firm—it should not be falling apart.

1 Heat the olive oil in a large saucepan, add the onions, leeks, chopped tomatoes, and garlic, and sauté over a low heat for a few minutes until soft, stirring frequently. Stir in the fennel, thyme, bay leaf, and orange peel.

PREPARATION: 20 MINUTES
COOKING: 30 MINUTES
SERVES: 6–8

MOULES MARINIERE
Sailor-style mussels

1 Put the mussels in a large bowl, cover with cold water and discard any that are open or cracked or rise to the surface. Scrub the mussels well with a stiff brush under cold running water to clean them thoroughly.

2 Melt the butter in a large saucepan, stir in the onion and garlic and fry gently until soft. Stir in the wine and then add the *bouquet garni* and bring to a boil. Boil for 2 minutes, add a pinch of salt and some black pepper to taste, and then add the mussels.

PREPARATION: 10–15 MINUTES
COOKING: 20 MINUTES
SERVES: 4–6

3 Cover the pan and cook over a high heat, shaking vigorously from time to time, until the mussel shells open. Remove from the pan with a slotted spoon and set aside. Discard any mussels that do not open.

7 cups fresh mussels in their shells
1/2 cup butter
1 onion, finely chopped
1 garlic clove, minced
1 1/2 cups dry white wine
1 *bouquet garni*
salt and freshly ground black pepper
2 tablespoons chopped parsley

4 Boil the liquid rapidly until reduced by half, then return the mussels to the pan and heat through for 1 minute, shaking the pan constantly. Sprinkle with the parsley and shake the pan again. Pile the mussels up in a warm deep serving dish or in individual dishes and pour the liquid over the top. Serve immediately with crusty bread.

COQUILLES DE FRUITS DE MER

Broiled seafood shells

1 Wash and scrub the mussels and place them in an ovenproof dish with a little water. Put in a preheated oven at 350° until they open. Remove the mussels from the shells, and separate the white parts and corals of the scallops.

2 Melt half of the butter in a skillet and sauté the onion, garlic, and mushrooms until they are lightly colored. Mix in the mussels and scallops and heat through gently.

PREPARATION: 30 MINUTES
COOKING: 15 MINUTES
SERVES: 4

3 Butter 4 deep scallop shells and sprinkle in half of the bread crumbs. Divide the seafood mixture between the shells. Boil up 4 tablespoons of water with the wine and lemon juice until reduced, and spoon over the shells.

2 cups fresh mussels in their shells
6 ounces queen scallops
¼ cup butter
1 tablespoon finely chopped onion
1 garlic clove, minced
½ cup sliced mushrooms
1 cup fresh white bread crumbs
⅔ cup dry white wine
1 tablespoon lemon juice
1 tablespoon chopped parsley
salt and freshly ground black pepper

4 Combine the remaining bread crumbs with the chopped parsley and seasoning and scatter over the shells. Melt the remaining butter and pour over the top. Place the filled shells on a cookie sheet and then bake in a preheated oven at 350° for 15 minutes, until golden brown.

BOEUF EN DAUBE PROVENCAL

Provençal beef stew

1 Put the cubes of beef in a deep bowl with 1 sliced onion, the carrots, orange peel, bay leaf, and peppercorns. Pour the red wine over the top, cover the bowl and leave to marinate in the refrigerator overnight. The following day, remove the meat and vegetables and drain well. Keep the marinade and vegetables.

3 Return the meat to the pan, together with the wine marinade, including the marinated vegetables, orange peel, and bay leaf. Discard the peppercorns. Add the stock, salt, and pepper, and bring to a boil.

2 Heat the oil or lard in a flame-proof casserole, add the meat and brown on all sides, stirring occasionally. Remove from the pan with a slotted spoon and keep warm. Add the remaining onion and the garlic to the casserole, and cook gently until golden brown.

2 pounds top round of beef, trimmed and cut into cubes
2 large onions, sliced
3 carrots, sliced
1 strip orange peel, without pith
1 bay leaf
4–5 peppercorns
1¼ cups red wine
¼ cup oil or lard
3 garlic cloves, minced
1¼ cups beef stock
salt and freshly ground black pepper

To garnish:

2 tablespoons finely chopped parsley

PREPARATION: 20 MINUTES + MARINATING OVERNIGHT
COOKING: 2–2½ HOURS
SERVES: 6

4 Cover the casserole and cook in a preheated oven at 325° for 2–2½ hours, until tender. Discard the bay leaf, and remove the meat from the casserole and keep warm. Boil the sauce until reduced by half. Return the meat to the casserole or place in another dish and pour the sauce over the top. Sprinkle with parsley and serve.

TOURNEDOS EN CROUTE

Prime steak in pastry crust

3 tablespoons butter
1 tablespoon oil
2 small onions, finely chopped
1 garlic clove, minced
1 cup chopped mushrooms
salt and freshly ground black pepper
pinch of ground nutmeg
4 prime steaks, about 6 ounces each, trimmed
½ pound fresh or frozen puff pastry
1 egg, beaten
4 slices ham

To garnish:

fresh chervil or parsley sprigs

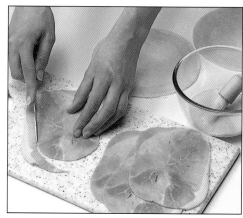

2 Heat the remaining butter in a clean skillet, add the steaks and then sear quickly on both sides. Remove from the skillet, cool quickly, and keep chilled until required.

3 Roll out the pastry on a lightly floured surface and cut into 8 circles, large enough to half cover the steaks. Brush a 1-inch border around the edge of each piece of pastry with beaten egg. Cut the ham into 8 round portions, the same size as the steaks.

1 Heat 2 tablespoons of the butter and the oil in a skillet and gently cook the onions and garlic until soft. Add the mushrooms, salt, pepper, and nutmeg and stir over a gentle heat until the mushrooms are cooked and the moisture has evaporated. Remove from the skillet, divide into 8 portions and leave to cool.

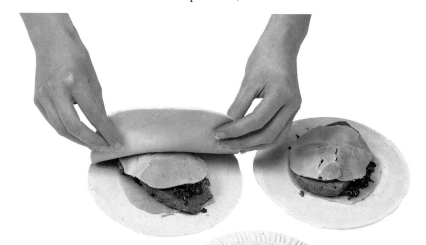

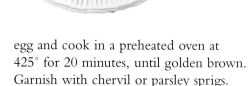

4 Place one piece of ham on each of 4 pastry circles. Cover the ham with a portion of the mushroom mixture, a prime steak, another portion of mushrooms, and another portion of ham. Top with a pastry circle. Seal the edges of the pastry between your fingers and then with a fork. Cut any pastry trimmings into leaves and use to decorate the *croûtes*. Brush with beaten egg and cook in a preheated oven at 425° for 20 minutes, until golden brown. Garnish with chervil or parsley sprigs.

PREPARATION: 30 MINUTES
COOKING: 30–35 MINUTES
SERVES: 4

BOEUF A LA BOURGUIGNONNE

Burgundy-style beef

1 large onion, thinly sliced
few sprigs of parsley
few sprigs of thyme
1 bay leaf, crushed
2 pounds top round of beef, cut into chunks
2 tablespoons **marc** or brandy
1³/4 cups red Burgundy wine
2 tablespoons olive oil
¹/4 cup butter
1 cup chopped bacon
24 small button onions, peeled
1 pound button mushrooms, halved
¹/4 cup all-purpose flour
1¹/4 cups beef stock
1 garlic clove, minced
1 *bouquet garni*
salt and freshly ground black pepper

1 Put a few onion slices in a deep bowl with a little parsley, thyme, and some crushed bay leaf. Place a few pieces of beef on top, and continue layering up in this way until all the onion, beef, and herbs are used. Mix together the *marc* or brandy with the wine and oil, and pour over the beef. Cover and leave to marinate for at least 4 hours.

3 Remove the beef from the marinade, then strain the marinade and set aside. Add the beef to the casserole and fry briskly until browned on all sides. Sprinkle in the flour and cook, stirring, for 1 minute. Gradually stir in the strained marinade, and then add the stock, garlic, and *bouquet garni*. Season to taste, cover the casserole and simmer gently for 2 hours.

2 Melt the butter in a flameproof casserole, add the bacon and fry over moderate heat until golden brown. Remove and set aside. Add the button onions and fry until golden all over. Remove and set aside. Add the mushrooms and fry, stirring, for 1 minute. Drain and set aside.

PREPARATION: 30 MINUTES +
4 HOURS MARINATING TIME
COOKING: 2¹/2 HOURS
SERVES: 4–6

4 Skim off any fat on the surface, and add the bacon, onions, and mushrooms to the casserole. Cover and simmer for 30 minutes, or until the beef is tender. Discard the *bouquet garni* and serve immediately.

59

GIGOT AU PISTOU

Leg of lamb with garlic stuffing

4–pound leg of lamb
$1/3$ cup butter
1 pound potatoes, peeled and cut into $1/4$-inch slices
5 tablespoons olive oil
freshly ground sea salt and black pepper
For the *pistou*:
$1/4$ pound bacon slices, chopped
3 garlic cloves, minced
2 teaspoons finely chopped fresh basil
1 tablespoon finely chopped fresh parsley
To garnish:
small sprigs of fresh rosemary

1 Make the *pistou*: mix together the chopped bacon, minced garlic, chopped fresh basil, and parsley in a small bowl.

3 Spread the lamb with $1/4$ cup of the butter and place in a roasting pan. Cook in a preheated oven at 350° for 2–2$1/2$ hours, according to how pink or well cooked you like your lamb.

2 Make an incision in the leg of lamb up to the bone and place the *pistou* mixture inside. Pull the sides of the meat together to enclose the stuffing. Sew it up with a trussing needle and thread.

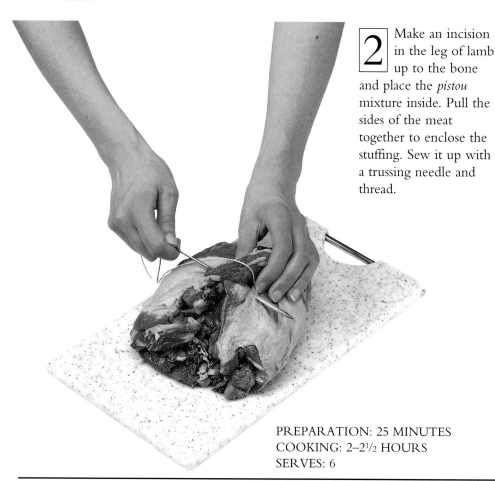

4 Add the potatoes to a pan of boiling salted water and cook for 4–5 minutes. Drain well. Just before the meat is cooked, heat the remaining butter and oil in a skillet and then sauté the potatoes, turning frequently, until crisp and golden. Season with salt and pepper. Remove the thread from the lamb. Serve garnished with sprigs of rosemary, and accompanied by the sautéed potatoes. If wished, you can use the meat juices to make gravy.

PREPARATION: 25 MINUTES
COOKING: 2–2$1/2$ HOURS
SERVES: 6

SAUTE DE PORC CATALANE

Catalan pork stew

⅔ cup olive oil

1½ pounds lean pork, cut into
1-inch cubes

1 large onion, sliced

2 garlic cloves, minced

1 pound tomatoes, skinned and chopped

1 sweet green pepper, seeded and chopped

1½ teaspoons paprika

⅔ cup chicken stock

salt and freshly ground black pepper

1 eggplant, sliced

2–3 tablespoons seasoned flour

To garnish:

chopped fresh cilantro leaves

2 Add the onion and garlic and cook until soft and golden. Return the meat to the pan, and stir in the tomatoes, sweet green pepper, paprika, and stock. Season with salt and freshly ground black pepper. Bring to a boil, cover with waxed paper and a lid, and simmer gently for 1 hour, or until the meat is tender.

1 Heat 2 tablespoons of the oil in a large saucepan or flameproof casserole, add the pork and sauté gently until golden brown on all sides, turning occasionally. Remove from the pan with a slotted spoon.

3 Meanwhile, sprinkle the eggplant slices with salt and leave them in a colander for at least 30 minutes to exude their bitter juice. Wash the eggplant and then pat dry with absorbent paper towels.

4 Dip the eggplant slices in seasoned flour. Heat some of the remaining oil in a large skillet. When it is hot, fry the eggplant slices, a few at a time, until they are golden brown on both sides. Add more oil as required. Remove with a slotted spoon and pat dry with absorbent towels. Serve the pork with the fried eggplant and plain boiled rice. Garnish with cilantro.

PREPARATION: 20 MINUTES
COOKING: 1¼ HOURS
SERVES: 4

PORC AUX PRUNEAUX DE TOURS

Pork Touraine-style

1 Soak the prunes in the white wine for several hours, or preferably leave them overnight. Put the soaked prunes in an ovenproof dish with 1¼ cups of the soaking liquid. Cover the dish and cook gently in a preheated oven at 300° for about 1 hour.

3 Add the remaining soaking liquid from the prunes, and the mushrooms to the skillet. Cover the skillet and cook gently over a low heat, at a bare simmer, for about 30 minutes. Turn the pork over halfway through the cooking time.

2 Coat the pork lightly on both sides with the flour seasoned with salt and black pepper. Heat the butter in a large skillet and sauté the pork until lightly browned on both sides.

PREPARATION: 20 MINUTES +
SOAKING OVERNIGHT
COOKING: 1¼ HOURS
SERVES: 4

10 ounces large prunes
1¾ cups dry white wine
4 pork noisettes or cutlets
2 tablespoons flour
salt and freshly ground black pepper
¼ cup butter
5 ounces button mushrooms
2 tablespoons cranberry jelly
¾ cup crème fraîche or light cream
To garnish:
3 tablespoons chopped parsley

4 Remove the pork and keep warm with the prunes. Add the remaining liquid in which the prunes were cooked to the skillet together with the cranberry jelly, and boil until the sauce reduces. Reduce the heat to a simmer and gradually stir in the crème fraîche or light cream. Heat very gently, without boiling, and adjust the seasoning. Serve the pork and prunes with the sauce, garnished with parsley.

CASSOULET TOULOUSAIN

Traditional stew from Toulouse

2¹/2 cups dried white haricot beans
³/4 pound belly pork, boned
1 small ham hock
2 carrots, thickly sliced
1 onion, peeled and stuck with 3 cloves
2 tomatoes, skinned and chopped
2 garlic cloves, minced
5 cups water
For the sauté:
3 tablespoons olive oil
³/4 pound lean lamb, cubed
2 onions, chopped
2 garlic cloves, minced
2 tomatoes, skinned and chopped
salt and freshly ground black pepper
1 *bouquet garni*
2 Toulouse or spicy sausages, thickly sliced
¹/2 pound *confit d'oie* (optional)
³/4 cup dried bread crumbs

1 Soak the beans in cold water overnight. Rinse and drain them the following day. Soak the belly pork and ham hock overnight to reduce the saltiness. Put the drained beans, pork and ham in a large saucepan with the carrots, onion, tomatoes, garlic, and water. Simmer gently for 2 hours, or until tender.

3 Ladle in sufficient cooking liquid from the bean pan to cover the lamb. Add the tomatoes, seasoning, and *bouquet garni*. Cover the skillet and simmer gently for 1¹/2 hours. Brown the sausages in a small skillet and then add to the lamb for a further 10 minutes.

2 Meanwhile, heat the olive oil in a large skillet and add the lamb. Sauté until lightly browned on all sides. Add the onions and garlic and sauté until soft and golden.

4 Remove the pork and ham and cut into chunks. Put half of the beans in a large ovenproof dish and add the chunks of ham and pork, the *confit d'oie* (if using) and the lamb mixture with its liquid. Cover with the remaining beans and sprinkle with bread crumbs. Bake in a preheated oven at 300° for 1 hour.

PREPARATION: 30 MINUTES +
SOAKING OVERNIGHT
COOKING: 3 HOURS
SERVES: 6–8

RIS DE VEAU A LA NORMANDE

Sweetbreads with mushrooms and cream

1 Soak the sweetbreads in a bowl of cold water for 3 hours, changing the water 2 or 3 times. Drain the sweetbreads and rinse thoroughly under running cold water. Put them in a saucepan, cover with fresh water and bring slowly to a boil. Simmer for 5 minutes, then drain and rinse again under running cold water.

2 Remove any fatty bits and then place the sweetbreads between 2 plates. Weight them down and leave for 1 hour. Melt half of the butter in a skillet. Slice the sweetbreads and add to the pan. Fry gently until they are lightly colored on both sides.

3 Coat the mushrooms with the flour, shaking off any excess, and add them to the skillet. Season with salt and pepper, then cover and simmer very gently for 15 minutes. Remove the sweetbreads and mushrooms with a slotted spoon and keep warm.

4 calves' sweetbreads
$^2/_3$ cup butter
$^1/_2$ pound mushrooms, sliced
2 tablespoons all-purpose flour
salt and freshly ground black pepper
7 tablespoons calvados or brandy
$^3/_4$ cup heavy cream
1 tablespoon chopped fresh parsley

PREPARATION: 10 MINUTES +
4 HOURS SOAKING TIME
COOKING: 30 MINUTES
SERVES: 4–6

4 Stir the calvados or brandy into the skillet and scrape up the sediment from the bottom. Stir in the cream and simmer over a very low heat until reduced by half. Remove from the heat and whisk in the remaining butter, a little at a time. Pour over the sweetbreads and mushrooms and serve sprinkled with parsley.

ROGNONS A LA BOURGUIGNONNE

Lamb's kidneys in Burgundy

2 tablespoons butter
1 tablespoon olive oil
1 onion, finely chopped
1 cup chopped mushrooms
2/3 cup diced bacon
8 lamb's kidneys
1¼ cups Burgundy or other dry red wine
salt and freshly ground black pepper
1 garlic clove, minced
1 *bouquet garni*
1 tablespoon flour
1 tablespoon chopped fresh parsley

1 Heat half of the butter and the oil in a heavy skillet. Add the onion, mushrooms, and bacon, and sauté gently until golden. Remove them from the skillet with a slotted spoon and keep warm.

2 Remove the skin surrounding the kidneys and trim away the fat. Split the kidneys in half lengthwise and, using a sharp knife, remove the central white cores. Add the prepared kidneys to the skillet and cook them over a high heat to seal them. Reduce the heat and cook gently for 3–4 minutes. Remove from the skillet and keep warm.

3 Add the red wine to the skillet together with the onion, mushroom, and bacon mixture. Season with salt and pepper, and stir in the garlic and *bouquet garni*. Simmer gently for 10 minutes.

4 Mix the remaining butter with the flour to make a *beurre manié*, and add to the sauce, a little at a time, stirring all the time until it thickens. Pour the sauce over the kidneys and serve sprinkled with parsley.

PREPARATION: 15 MINUTES
COOKING: 25 MINUTES
SERVES: 4

COQ AU VIN
Chicken in red wine

2 tablespoons oil
¼ cup butter
1 x 5-pound chicken, cut into 12 serving pieces
24 small button onions, peeled
1 cup diced bacon
1 tablespoon all-purpose flour
1 bottle good red wine, e.g. Burgundy
1 *bouquet garni*
2 garlic cloves
pinch of sugar
pinch of ground nutmeg
salt and freshly ground black pepper
24 button mushrooms
1 tablespoon brandy
3–4 slices bread
oil for frying
2 tablespoons chopped parsley

3 Add the mushrooms and continue cooking gently for a further 45 minutes, or until the chicken is cooked and tender. Remove the chicken with a slotted spoon and arrange the pieces on a warm serving platter. Keep hot. Pour the brandy into the sauce and boil, uncovered, for 5 minutes until thick and reduced. Remove the *bouquet garni* and garlic cloves.

1 Heat the oil and butter in a large flameproof casserole and add the chicken pieces. Fry gently over a low heat until golden on all sides, turning occasionally. Remove with a slotted spoon and keep warm. Pour off a little of the fat from the casserole, then add the onions and bacon. Sauté until lightly colored, then sprinkle in the flour and stir well.

PREPARATION: 15–20 MINUTES
COOKING: 1½ HOURS
SERVES: 6

2 Pour in the wine and bring to a boil, stirring. Add the *bouquet garni*, unpeeled garlic cloves, sugar, nutmeg, and salt and pepper to taste. Return the chicken to the casserole, lower the heat, cover and simmer for 15 minutes.

4 Remove the crusts from the bread and cut into pieces. Fry in oil until crisp and golden on both sides. Remove and pat with absorbent paper towels. Pour the sauce over the chicken and serve with the bread *croûtes*. Sprinkle with chopped parsley.

POULET BASQUAISE

Basque-style chicken

1 Heat the olive oil in a sauté pan or deep skillet. Add the diced bacon or ham and sauté gently, stirring occasionally, until lightly browned. Remove the bacon with a slotted spoon and keep warm.

3 Add the tomatoes and some stock (1¼ cups for fresh tomatoes; ⅔ cup for canned tomatoes in juice). Season with salt and pepper. Return the chicken and ham to the skillet, cover and cook gently for 40–45 minutes, or until the chicken is cooked and tender.

2 Add the chicken portions to the skillet and cook, turning occasionally, until they are brown all over. Remove with a slotted spoon and keep warm. Add the onions and garlic and cook gently until soft and golden. Add the sweet peppers and marjoram, cover, and cook gently for 10 minutes.

4 tablespoons olive oil
1⅓ cups diced bacon or ham
4 large chicken portions
4 onions, sliced
3 garlic cloves, minced
2 sweet green peppers, seeded and diced
¼ teaspoon dried marjoram
¾ pound fresh or canned tomatoes, skinned
⅔–1¼ cups chicken stock
salt and freshly ground black pepper
2 tablespoons chopped fresh parsley

4 Remove the chicken and transfer to a serving dish. Boil the sauce gently to reduce it if necessary, until it is thick enough to coat the back of a spoon. Adjust the seasoning and pour over the chicken. Sprinkle with chopped parsley and serve.

PREPARATION: 20 MINUTES
COOKING: 1 HOUR
SERVES: 4

CANARD A L'ORANGE

Duck with oranges

2 tablespoons butter

3 tablespoons olive oil

1 x 4-pound duck, trussed with thread

4 garlic cloves, minced

1/4 pound raw country ham, cut into thin strips

2 1/2 cups dry white wine

3/4 cup chicken stock

1 *bouquet garni*

salt and freshly ground black pepper

1 tablespoon wine vinegar

pared peel and juice of 2 oranges

For the beurre manié:

1 tablespoon all-purpose flour

2 tablespoons softened butter

To garnish:

2 oranges, cut into thin slices

2 Add the garlic and strips of ham to the casserole and fry for 1–2 minutes. Pour in the white wine and stock, bring to the boil and then simmer for a few minutes until slightly reduced. Add the *bouquet garni*, salt and pepper, and orange juice, and then cover the casserole. Reduce the heat and simmer gently for 1 1/2 hours, or until the duck is cooked. Baste occasionally during cooking.

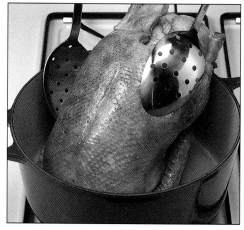

1 Heat the butter and oil in a deep flameproof casserole and add the duck. Fry over a medium heat, turning the duck as necesssary, until it is golden brown all over.

PREPARATION: 20 MINUTES
COOKING: 1 1/2 HOURS
SERVES: 6

3 Using a sharp knife, cut the pared orange peel into fine strips, and plunge them into a small pan of boiling water. Blanch for 5 minutes, then remove and drain. Dry thoroughly on absorbent paper towels and set aside.

4 Make the *beurre manié:* blend the flour and butter. Remove the cooked duck from the casserole, cut into serving pieces and keep warm. Boil the cooking liquid for about 10 minutes, until reduced. Add the vinegar, strips of orange peel, and little pieces of *beurre manié,* stirring all the time, until the sauce thickens. Serve the duck with the orange sauce, garnished with orange slices.

SALADE DE LENTILLES TIEDE

Warm lentil salad

1 Put the lentils in a bowl, cover with water and leave to soak for 3–4 hours. Drain well and put them in a large saucepan.

3 Slice the remaining carrot thinly and blanch in a saucepan of lightly salted boiling water with the leek and celery. Drain well.

2 Peel one of the carrots and add to the lentils in the saucepan, together with the onion studded with the clove, the bay leaf, thyme, and garlic. Cover with cold water and bring to a boil, then simmer for 30–35 minutes. Remove and discard the vegetables, bay leaf, and garlic, and drain the lentils.

PREPARATION: 10 MINUTES +
3–4 HOURS SOAKING TIME
COOKING: 45 MINUTES
SERVES: 4

1½ cups green lentils
2 carrots
1 onion, peeled
1 clove
1 bay leaf
pinch of dried thyme
1 garlic clove, minced
1 leek, thinly sliced
⅓ cup chopped celery
1⅓ cups diced bacon
1 tablespoon oil
1 tablespoon snipped chives
For the vinaigrette:
¾ cup walnut oil
6 tablespoons sherry or wine vinegar
1 tablespoon Dijon mustard
salt and pepper

4 Meanwhile, whisk the ingredients together for the vinaigrette dressing, and fry the bacon in the oil until crisp. Stir the blanched vegetables and fried bacon gently into the lentils and toss in the vinaigrette dressing. Sprinkle with snipped chives and serve warm.

SALADE NICOISE

Tuna salad from Nice

1 Rub around the inside of a large salad bowl with the bruised garlic clove. Line the bowl with lettuce leaves. Chop the remaining lettuce leaves roughly and then arrange them in the bottom of the bowl.

2 Mix together the celery and cucumber with the green beans and artichoke hearts. Arrange on top of the lettuce in the salad bowl.

3 Arrange the quartered tomatoes, sliced sweet pepper, onion, eggs, olives, and anchovies on top of the mixed vegetables in the bowl. Cut the tuna into chunks and place in the bowl.

1 garlic clove, peeled and bruised
1 lettuce, separated into leaves
1/4 pound celery hearts, thinly sliced
1/4 pound cucumber, peeled and thinly sliced
1/2 pound thin green beans, topped and tailed
1/2 pound canned artichoke hearts, thinly sliced
1 pound tomatoes, skinned, seeded and quartered
1 large sweet green pepper, seeded and sliced
1 onion, sliced
4 hard-boiled eggs, halved
1/2 cup ripe olives
8 canned anchovy fillets, drained
1 x 8-ounce can tuna fish in oil, drained

For the dressing:
7 tablespoons olive oil
4 basil leaves, finely chopped
salt and freshly ground black pepper

4 Make the dressing: mix together the olive oil and chopped basil with the seasoning. Pour the dressing over the salad and transfer to individual serving plates.

PREPARATION: 20 MINUTES
SERVES: 4

RATATOUILLE NICOISE

Vegetable stew from Nice

3 Add the zucchini and continue frying for 5–6 minutes until they are lightly colored. Remove the eggplants and zucchini from the pan with a slotted spoon, and set aside.

1 Make a small incision in each tomato with a sharp knife. Put them in a bowl and cover with boiling water. Leave for 1–2 minutes, then remove and skin the tomatoes. Chop them roughly.

1½ pounds tomatoes
½ cup olive oil
1 pound eggplants, thinly sliced or diced
1 pound zucchini, sliced
1 pound onions, thinly sliced
1 pound sweet green peppers, seeded and thinly sliced
5 garlic cloves, minced
salt and freshly ground black pepper
2 sprigs of thyme
5 basil leaves

To garnish:

1 tablespoon chopped parsley

PREPARATION: 30 MINUTES
COOKING: 40 MINUTES
SERVES: 6

2 Heat half of the oil in a large heavy saucepan and add the eggplants. Fry them gently over a moderate heat until they are lightly golden, stirring frequently.

4 Add the remaining oil to the pan. Stir in the onions and fry gently until soft and golden. Add the sweet peppers and garlic, increase the heat and fry for 3–4 minutes. Add the tomatoes and cook gently for 10 minutes. Stir in the eggplants and zucchini, season to taste, and crumble in the thyme. Cook gently, uncovered, for about 40 minutes. Crumble the basil leaves into the ratatouille, and serve it warm or cold, garnished with parsley.

GALETTES DE POMMES DE TERRE
Potato cakes

1 Peel the potatoes and grate them coarsely with a grater or in a food processor. Put the grated potatoes in a sieve and rinse well under running cold water. Drain and transfer the potatoes to a bowl.

2 Break the eggs into the bowl of grated potatoes and mix together. Add the chopped onions, flour, herbs, and garlic. Season with salt and pepper and a little ground nutmeg, and stir the mixture thoroughly.

3 Divide the potato mixture into equal-sized portions and mold them into small cakes, using a spoon to shape them.

2 pounds potatoes
3 eggs
$2/3$ cup chopped onions
1 tablespoon flour
1 tablespoon chopped parsley and chives
1 garlic clove, minced
salt and pepper
pinch of ground nutmeg
6 tablespoons oil

4 Heat the oil in a skillet. When it is hot, add the potato cakes and fry until golden brown and crisp on both sides, turning them once during cooking. Serve them very hot with a meat dish, or with some cold meats and a green salad.

PREPARATION: 20 MINUTES
COOKING: 5–10 MINUTES
SERVES: 4

GRATIN D'ASPERGES AU JAMBON

Asparagus and ham au gratin

1 Cook the asparagus for 15–20 minutes in boiling salted water to which the lemon juice and sugar have been added. The asparagus should be tender but still firm. Let cool in the cooking liquid.

2 Put the cream and stock in a small saucepan and boil until reduced by half. Season to taste with salt and pepper and a little ground nutmeg. Remove the pan from the heat.

3 Drain the asparagus carefully so as not to damage the delicate stalks. Divide them into 4 equal-sized bundles and roll each one in a slice of ham. Arrange the ham bundles in a buttered ovenproof dish.

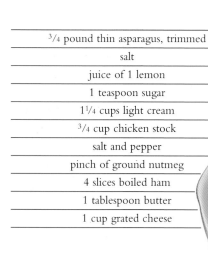

4 Pour the reduced cream mixture over the top and sprinkle with the grated cheese. Bake in a preheated oven at 400° for 20–25 minutes, until bubbling and golden brown. Serve immediately.

3/4 pound thin asparagus, trimmed
salt
juice of 1 lemon
1 teaspoon sugar
1¼ cups light cream
3/4 cup chicken stock
salt and pepper
pinch of ground nutmeg
4 slices boiled ham
1 tablespoon butter
1 cup grated cheese

PREPARATION: 20–25 MINUTES
COOKING: 20–25 MINUTES
SERVES: 4

FARCIS PROVENCAUX

Provençal stuffed vegetables

1 Cut the eggplants in half lengthwise, scoop out and keep the flesh. Plunge the onions into boiling water for a few minutes, drain and hollow out the centers, reserving the scooped-out flesh. Cut a hole in the top of each tomato, scoop out the flesh and keep. Sprinkle some salt, pepper, and a little of the olive oil inside the hollow vegetables.

2 Prepare the stuffing: mix together in a bowl the veal or pork, onion, garlic, parsley, and the flesh from the hollowed-out vegetables.

3 Heat 1 tablespoon of olive oil in a skillet and add the stuffing mixture. Fry gently for 4–5 minutes, stirring constantly. Remove the skillet from the heat and then stir in the Parmesan cheese, rice, and thyme. Stir in the beaten eggs and season to taste with salt and pepper.

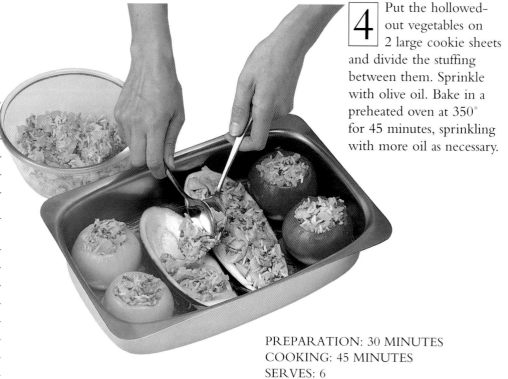

4 Put the hollowed-out vegetables on 2 large cookie sheets and divide the stuffing between them. Sprinkle with olive oil. Bake in a preheated oven at 350° for 45 minutes, sprinkling with more oil as necessary.

3 eggplants
6 large onions
6 large tomatoes
salt and freshly ground black pepper
7 tablespoons olive oil
For the stuffing:
³/₄ pound ground veal or pork
1 onion, finely chopped
2 garlic cloves, minced
few parsley sprigs, chopped
2 tablespoons grated Parmesan cheese
2 tablespoons boiled long-grain rice
2 sprigs of thyme, crumbled
2 eggs, beaten

PREPARATION: 30 MINUTES
COOKING: 45 MINUTES
SERVES: 6

GRATIN DAUPHINOIS

Layered creamy potatoes

1 garlic clove, peeled

1/3 cup softened butter

2 pounds waxy potatoes

salt and freshly ground black pepper

pinch of ground nutmeg

1 1/2 cups hot milk

1 1/4 cups light cream

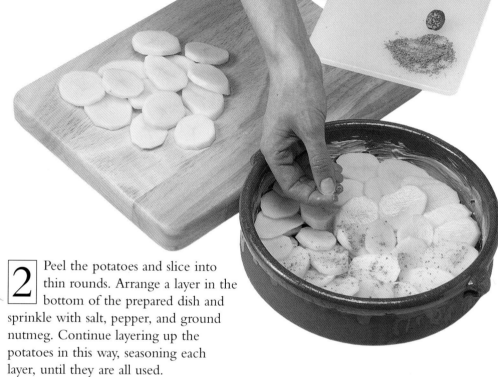

1 Cut the garlic clove in half and use it to rub round the inside of a large earthenware baking dish to exude its flavor and aroma to the finished dish. Brush the dish thickly with some of the softened butter.

2 Peel the potatoes and slice into thin rounds. Arrange a layer in the bottom of the prepared dish and sprinkle with salt, pepper, and ground nutmeg. Continue layering up the potatoes in this way, seasoning each layer, until they are all used.

3 Mix the hot milk and cream together, and then pour the mixture over the layered potatoes, making sure that the potatoes are almost totally covered by the liquid.

4 Dot the top with the remaining butter and bake in a preheated oven at 350° for 1–1 1/4 hours, or until the potatoes are tender when pierced with a skewer. Increase the oven temperature to 400° for the last 10 minutes of cooking time to brown the top layer of potatoes. Serve hot, straight from the baking dish.

PREPARATION: 15–20 MINUTES

COOKING: 1–1 1/4 HOURS

SERVES: 4–6

TIAN

Provençal baked vegetables

1 Put the eggplant slices in a colander and sprinkle with salt. Leave for 30 minutes to exude their bitter juices. Rinse well under running cold water and pat dry.

2 Sauté the sliced eggplant with the onions, sweet peppers, and garlic in 4 tablespoons of olive oil until golden. Spread the mixture over the base of a shallow oval ovenproof dish.

1 eggplant, sliced
salt
2 onions, thinly sliced
2 sweet red peppers, seeded and sliced
4 garlic cloves, minced
6 tablespoons olive oil
2 large zucchini
3 large tomatoes
freshly ground black pepper
sprigs of fresh thyme and rosemary
3 tablespoons fresh white bread crumbs
2 tablespoons grated Parmesan cheese

4 Remove the dish from the oven and sprinkle with the bread crumbs and Parmesan. Drizzle a little more olive oil over the top if wished. Bake for a further 10 minutes until crisp and golden. Eat hot, warm, or cold.

3 Using a potato peeler, remove some of the peel in strips from the sides of the zucchini, leaving some vertical stripes of green. Slice the zucchini thinly. Slice the tomatoes. Arrange the zucchini and tomato slices in alternate rows over the top of the sautéed vegetable mixture, overlapping them like fish scales. Season to taste with some salt and pepper and add a few sprigs of thyme and rosemary. Bake in a preheated oven at 375° for 25 minutes, until golden.

PREPARATION: 45 MINUTES
COOKING: 25 MINUTES
SERVES: 4

OEUFS A LA NEIGE AU CITRON

Lemon snow eggs

1 Put the egg whites in a large clean bowl and whisk well until they form firm peaks. Gradually whisk in ½ cup of the sugar. Fold in the grated lemon peel.

2 Beat the egg yolks together and add 2 tablespoons of the cold milk. Bring the rest of the milk to a boil in a large saucepan, add the strip of lemon peel, and stir in the remaining sugar. Reduce the heat.

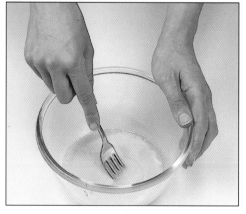

3 Drop teaspoons of the beaten egg white into the hot milk and poach gently for 2 minutes. Remove with a slotted spoon, drain on absorbent paper towels, and set aside while you make the lemon custard.

5 eggs, separated
finely grated peel of ½ lemon
2½ cups milk
strip of lemon peel
¾ cup sugar

4 Cool the milk and stir in the beaten egg yolks. Heat the mixture gently in a double boiler, or a basin, over simmering water, stirring continuously until the custard thickens. Do not allow to boil. Remove the lemon peel and let the custard cool down. Pour into a shallow serving dish and float the meringues on top. Chill well before serving.

PREPARATION: 15-20 MINUTES
COOKING: 20-30 MINUTES
SERVES: 4

TARTE AUX POMMES ALSACIENNE

Alsace-style apple tart

2 tablespoons butter
1/2 pound *pâte brisée* (see page 110)
2 pounds green dessert apples
2/3 cup sugar
1 teaspoon ground cinnamon
3 tablespoons milk
2/3 cup light cream
2 eggs
2 tablespoons confectioners' sugar

1 Butter a 10-inch loose-bottomed quiche pan and line with the *pâte brisée* (short-crust pastry). Prick the base of the pastry shell all over with a fork.

2 Peel, core, and quarter the apples. Slice the quartered apples without separating the slices and spread them out fan-fashion in the pastry shell in an attractive pattern.

3 Sprinkle the apples with 2 tablespoons of the sugar and then with the ground cinnamon. Bake in a preheated oven at 400° for 20 minutes.

4 Mix the remaining sugar in a bowl with the milk, cream, and eggs. Beat lightly and then pour over the cooked apples. Return to the oven for a further 10–15 minutes. When the tart is cooked and the custard set, dust with confectioners' sugar and serve warm.

PREPARATION: 20 MINUTES
COOKING: 30–35 MINUTES
SERVES: 6–8

CREPES SUZETTE

Sweet orange crêpes

For the batter:

1 cup all-purpose flour
¼ teaspoon salt
3 eggs
2 tablespoons oil
¼ cup melted butter
1 tablespoon sugar
2 teaspoons vanilla sugar
1½ cups milk
2 tablespoons butter for frying

For the syrup:

½ cup softened butter, diced
½ cup sugar
grated peel and juice of 1 orange
6 tablespoons Cointreau or Grand Marnier
3 tablespoons brandy

2 Melt a little of the butter in a small skillet and, when it is really hot, ladle some of the batter into the skillet. Tilt the skillet so that the batter covers the base evenly and fry until golden brown on the underside. Flip the crêpe over and cook the other side. Slide onto a warm plate and cook the other crêpes.

3 Make the syrup: put the butter and sugar in a bowl and beat together until smooth and creamy. Beat the orange peel and juice into the creamed mixture, and then beat in 3 tablespoons of the orange liqueur and 1 tablespoon of the brandy.

4 Transfer the orange mixture to a large skillet and heat gently. Boil rapidly for 1–2 minutes, and reduce the heat. Add the crêpes, one at a time, folding each one in half and then in half again. Simmer gently until hot. Warm the remaining liqueur and brandy in a small pan, set alight and pour flaming over the crêpes just before serving. Alternatively, cook the crêpes and set alight at the table.

1 Make the batter: sift the flour and salt into a bowl and make a well in the center. Tip in the eggs, oil, melted butter, sugars, and milk, and beat until smooth, using a hand-held electric whisk if wished.

PREPARATION: 25 MINUTES
COOKING: 6–8 MINUTES
SERVES: 6–8

TARTE AU FROMAGE BLANC

Cheesecake

1 Put the raisins in a small bowl with the Kirsch. Leave to soak while you prepare the cheesecake. Line a 9-inch loose-bottomed quiche pan with the *pâte brisée* (short-crust pastry). Prick the base with a fork.

3 Pour the cream cheese filling into the short-crust pastry shell. Sprinkle the surface with the soaked raisins. Place in a preheated oven at 350°

2 Put the *fromage blanc* in a bowl and mix in the cream and sugar. Gently beat in the egg yolks, arrowroot or cornstarch, and lemon rind. Beat the egg whites until stiff and fold gently into the mixture.

PREPARATION: 20 MINUTES
COOKING: 50 MINUTES
SERVES: 6

¹/₄ cup raisins
1 tablespoon Kirsch
¹/₂ pound *pâte brisée* (see page 110)
¹/₂ pound *fromage blanc* or soft cheese
3 tablespoons light cream
¹/₂ cup sugar
3 eggs, separated
2 tablespoons arrowroot or cornstarch
grated rind of 1 lemon
confectioners' sugar for dusting

4 After 10 minutes, lower the oven temperature to 300°, and bake for a further 40 minutes. The cheesecake is cooked when the blade of a knife inserted into it comes out dry. Remove from the pan and cool. When cold, dust with confectioners' sugar, and then serve.

CREME CARAMEL

Caramel custard

| 2 cups milk |
| 1 vanilla bean, split in half lengthwise |
| 4 eggs |
| 1/4 cup sugar |
| **For the caramel:** |
| 1/4 cup sugar |
| 1 tablespoon water |
| 1 teaspoon lemon juice |

1 Put the milk and vanilla bean in a heavy saucepan and bring to a boil. Remove from the heat and leave for 5 minutes to infuse. Whisk the eggs and sugar together in a bowl until thoroughly combined. Discard the vanilla and whisk the milk into the egg and sugar mixture.

3 Pour the caramel into 6 small molds or 1 large 1³/4-pint charlotte mold. Rotate the molds quickly so that the caramel coats the base and sides evenly.

4 Strain the custard through a fine sieve. Pour into the molds and stand in a roasting pan half-filled with water (*bain marie*). Cook in a preheated oven at 300° for about 45 minutes, or until set. Leave to cool and then chill in the refrigerator before unmolding. To unmold, dip the base of the molds into a bowl of hot water for 30 seconds and then turn out on to a serving plate.

2 While the milk is infusing, make the caramel. Put the sugar, water, and lemon juice in a small saucepan and cook over moderate heat, stirring well until the sugar dissolves. When it turns a rich golden caramel color, remove from the heat immediately.

PREPARATION: 15 MINUTES
COOKING: 45 MINUTES
SERVES: 4–5

TARTE TATIN

Upside-down apple tart

1 Make the caramel: put the sugar and water in a flameproof oval or round baking dish and place over a low heat. Stir well to dissolve the sugar completely, then turn up the heat and cook until the sugar starts to caramelize and turns golden brown. Remove quickly from the heat and stir in the butter. Add a little hot water if necessary to thin the caramel, standing well back.

3 pounds crisp dessert apples
1/3 cup sugar
1/3 cup butter
1/2 pound fresh or frozen puff pastry
For the caramel:
1/3 cup sugar
3 tablespoons water
2 tablespoons butter

2 Peel and core the apples. Cut each one in half and pack tightly into the dish, arranging them in concentric circles so that each round side fits neatly into a hollowed-out side.

3 Sprinkle the apples with the sugar. Cut the butter into small dice and scatter across the top of the apples in the dish. Cook in the preheated oven at 375° for about 20 minutes.

4 Roll out the puff pastry on a lightly floured board and place on top of the apples. Tuck in the pastry edges around the side of the dish. Increase the oven temperature to 425° and bake for a further 15–20 minutes, until the pastry is well-risen and golden brown. Cool a little and then invert the tart on to a serving platter. Serve warm with cream or crème fraîche.

PREPARATION: 20 MINUTES
COOKING: 35–40 MINUTES
SERVES: 6

PARIS-BREST

Choux ring with praline cream filling

For the choux pastry:

¼ cup butter

⅔ cup water

pinch of salt

⅓ cup all-purpose flour, sifted

2 large eggs

¼ cup slivered almonds

confectioners' sugar for dusting

For the praline cream:

½ cup blanched almonds

⅓ cup sugar

1¼ cups heavy cream, whipped

2 Beat in the eggs, one at a time, and then put the choux paste in a pastry bag fitted with a ½-inch plain tip. Pipe a ring, 8 inches in diameter, on to a greased cookie sheet, then another ring inside the first one, and a ring on top. Sprinkle with almonds and bake in a preheated oven at 400° for 30 minutes, or until well-risen and golden brown. Cool on a wire rack.

1 Make the choux pastry: put the butter, water, and salt in a medium-sized saucepan and bring to a boil. Tip in the sifted flour all at once and remove from the heat. Beat with a wooden spoon until the choux paste is smooth and leaves the sides of the pan clean.

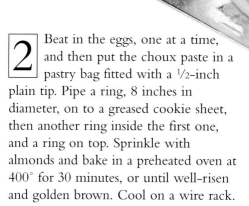

3 Make the praline: put the blanched almonds and sugar in a small heavy-bottomed saucepan, and stir over a gentle heat until the sugar melts and caramelizes and the almonds are toasted.

4 Pour the mixture on to an oiled cookie sheet, and set aside until cold and crisp. Grind to a fine powder in a food processor or electric grinder, and mix into the whipped cream. Split the choux ring horizontally, and fill with the praline cream. Place the top in position and serve the choux ring dusted with confectioners' sugar.

PREPARATION: 30 MINUTES
COOKING: 30 MINUTES
SERVES: 6

TARTE CITRON

Lemon tart

1 Make the pastry: sift the flour and salt into a bowl and rub in the butter until the mixture resembles bread crumbs. Stir in the egg yolk and sufficient iced water to make a soft and pliable dough. Chill in the refrigerator for 30 minutes.

2 Make the filling: put the lemon peel and juice, and sugar in a mixing bowl. Break in the eggs and add the egg white. Beat well together and then beat in the cream, ground almonds, and cinnamon. The mixture should be thick and smooth.

PREPARATION: 15 MINUTES + 30 MINUTES CHILLING TIME
COOKING: 30 MINUTES
SERVES: 6-8

3 Roll out the pastry on a lightly floured surface, and use to line a 10-inch loose-bottomed quiche pan. Prick the base with a fork and pour in the filling mixture. Bake in a preheated oven at 375° for 30 minutes, or until it is set and golden. Set aside to cool.

2¼ cups all-purpose flour
pinch of salt
½ cup butter
1 egg yolk
2–3 tablespoons iced water

For the filling:
grated peel and juice of 3 lemons
⅓ cup sugar
2 eggs + 1 egg white
⅓ cup heavy cream
1 cup ground almonds
good pinch of ground cinnamon

For the topping:
2 lemons, thinly sliced
½ cup sugar

4 Heat the lemon slices in a little water over low heat for 10 minutes, or until tender. Remove and drain the lemon slices, keeping about ⅓ cup of the liquid. Add the sugar and stir over gentle heat until dissolved. Bring to a boil, add the lemon slices and cook rapidly until they are well coated with thick syrup. Remove and use to decorate the tart. Let cool, and then serve.

SAUCES AND PASTRY

AIOLI
Garlic sauce

8 cloves garlic, peeled
salt
2 egg yolks
1¼ cups olive oil
freshly ground black pepper
few drops of lemon juice

Crush the garlic with a little salt in a mortar. Place the egg yolks in a bowl and beat with the garlic. Add the olive oil, drop by drop, beating well between each addition. When the mixture thickens and becomes more creamy, you can add the remaining oil in a thin steady stream, beating all the time. Add a little ground black pepper and lemon juice and check the seasoning. You can store the aioli for a few days in a screwtop jar or sealed container in the refrigerator. Makes 1½ cups.

VINAIGRETTE
French oil and vinegar dressing

6 tablespoons olive oil
2 tablespoons white wine vinegar
1 teaspoon Dijon mustard
pinch of sugar
salt and freshly ground black pepper

Put the olive oil and wine vinegar in a bowl and mix with a fork. Whisk in the mustard and sugar until the mixture is thoroughly blended. Season with salt and pepper, and use as a dressing for salads and warm vegetables.

Variation: You can omit the mustard, or add minced garlic or chopped fresh herbs of your choice.

ROUILLE
Sweet red pepper sauce

1 small sweet red pepper
2 garlic cloves, minced
pinch of saffron powder
salt and freshly ground black pepper
2 ounces crustless white bread
2 egg yolks
1 cup olive oil

Cut the sweet pepper in half and remove the ribs and seeds. Chop the flesh into small pieces and crush to a paste with the garlic in a mortar. Add the saffron and salt and pepper to taste. Moisten the bread with a little water or some of the cooking liquid if making bouillabaisse (the traditional accompaniment for rouille). Work it into the sweet peppers and garlic until thoroughly incorporated. Beat in the egg yolks. Add the oil, a little at a time, beating well between each addition. As the rouille becomes thick, pour the oil in a thin steady stream. Continue beating until the rouille is really thick and smooth. Makes 1¼ cups.

PATE BRISEE
Short-crust pastry

2 cups all-purpose flour
⅓ cup butter, cut into small pieces
1 egg
pinch of salt
4–6 tablespoons water
¼ cup sugar (optional)

Sift the flour into a large bowl, and rub in the butter with your fingertips until the mixture resembles fine bread crumbs.

Add the egg, salt, and sufficient water to mix to a soft dough. If making sweet pastry for a fruit pie or flan, you can mix in the sugar and some extra water. Wrap the dough in plastic wrap and rest in the refrigerator for at least 30 minutes before using. The dough can be stored in this way in the refrigerator for up to 2 days.

Note: Alternatively, the pastry can be made in a food processor.

SAUCE BEARNAISE
Creamy tarragon sauce

1 cup butter, cut into small pieces
7 tablespoons white wine vinegar
½ onion, finely chopped
¼ teaspoon freshly ground white pepper
2 tablespoons chopped tarragon
3 egg yolks
2 tablespoons water
salt

Clarify the butter (as described in the recipe for *sauce hollandaise* on page 111). Put the vinegar in a saucepan with the onion, pepper, and half of the tarragon. Boil rapidly until the liquid has reduced to 1 tablespoon. Strain the reduced liquid into a clean pan and stand it in a water bath (*bain marie*).

Add the egg yolks to the strained liquid, one at a time, whisking vigorously. Whisk in the water, and then the clarified butter, a little at a time, until the sauce is like thick cream. Add the remaining tarragon and salt to taste. Serve with broiled steak or roast beef.

SAUCE HOLLANDAISE

1 cup butter, cut into small pieces
2 tablespoons white wine vinegar
4 tablespoons water
1/4 teaspoon freshly ground white pepper
3 egg yolks
1–2 tablespoons lemon juice
salt

First clarify the butter: put it in a heavy pan and melt over a very low heat. Skim off the white foam that rises to the surface, and strain the clear yellow liquid into a bowl.

Put the vinegar in a heavy pan with 2 tablespoons of water and the white pepper. Boil rapidly until the liquid has reduced to 1 teaspoon. Remove from the heat and stand the pan in a larger saucepan or a roasting pan half-filled with water (a *bain marie*). Stir 1 tablespoon of water into the reduced liquid and then add the egg yolks, one at a time, whisking vigorously after each addition.

Whisk in the clarified butter, a little at a time. Then whisk in the remaining water. The consistency of the sauce should be like thick cream. Pass the sauce through a sieve or conical strainer and then whisk in the lemon juice and salt to taste. Serve with cooked fish dishes and vegetables, especially asparagus.

Variation: To make a *sauce mousseline*, fold 2 tablespoons of lightly whipped cream into the hollandaise sauce just before serving.

BECHAMEL SAUCE
White sauce

2 1/2 cups milk
1 onion stuck with 2 cloves
1 carrot, quartered
1 *bouquet garni*
1/4 cup butter
1/2 cup all-purpose flour
salt and freshly ground white pepper
freshly ground nutmeg

Pour the milk into a saucepan and add the onion, carrot, and *bouquet garni*. Bring to a boil and then reduce the heat to a bare simmer. Leave the saucepan over a very low heat for 30 minutes to infuse. Melt the butter in a clean saucepan and stir in the flour.

Cook for 1 minute, stirring constantly to obtain a smooth *roux* (paste). Do not allow the *roux* to brown. Remove the pan from the heat and gradually stir in the milk, a little at a time, stirring vigorously after each addition. The sauce should be smooth without any lumps.

Return to the heat and bring slowly to the boil, stirring constantly. Lower the heat and simmer gently for 5–6 minutes, until the sauce thickens. Season with salt, pepper, and ground nutmeg.

Variation: Vary the flavor by adding chopped fresh herbs, such as tarragon, parsley, or chervil. Or you can add up to 1 1/4 cups freshly made tomato sauce for a *sauce aurore* to serve with fish, chicken, and egg dishes.

MAYONNAISE

1 egg yolk
1/2–2/3 cup olive oil
pinch of salt
3–4 teaspoons white wine vinegar or lemon juice

Before you make the mayonnaise, ensure that all the ingredients and utensils are at room temperature. Put the egg yolk in a bowl and beat with a whisk. Add the olive oil to the egg yolk, drop by drop at first, beating all the time. As the mayonnaise starts to thicken, start adding the oil faster in a thin, steady stream. Continue beating throughout until all the oil is absorbed. Add salt to taste, and blend in the vinegar or lemon juice. Serve at room temperature. Makes 3/4 cup mayonnaise.

Variation: If you like a mustard-flavored mayonnaise, add 1 teaspoon Dijon mustard to the egg yolk before adding the olive oil.

Important: If the mayonnaise starts to curdle, quickly whisk in 1 tablespoon boiling water. If this does not do the trick, you can start again with another egg yolk in a clean bowl. Add the curdled mayonnaise mixture, one drop at a time, beating well. Add the remaining olive oil, drop by drop, and then in a thin stream.

INDEX